A LITTLE GIANT® BOOK

SUPER SILLIEST RIDDLES

A LITTLE GIANT® BOOK

SUPER SILLIEST RIDDLES

Hold On to Your Head,
'Cause You Might Just Laugh It Off

Chris Tait, Jacqueline Horsfall
& Morrie Gallant

STERLING

New York / London
www.sterlingpublishing.com/kids

Library of Congress Cataloging-in-Publication Data Available

2 4 6 8 10 9 7 5 3 1

Published by Sterling Publishing Co., Inc.
387 Park Avenue South, New York, NY 10016
Illustrated by Buck Jones, Mark Zahnd, Rob Collinet, Sanford Hoffman,
Lance Lekander. and Jackie Snider.

Material in this collection was adapted from *Funniest Riddle Book in the World*
(text © by Morrie Gallant, illustrations by Sanford Hoffman), *Kids' Silliest
Riddles* (text © by Jacqueline Horsfall, illustrations by Buck Jones), *Ridiculous
Riddles* (text © by Chris Tait, illustrations by Mark Zahnd), *Kids' Kookiest
Riddles* (illustrations by Rob Collinet), *Dr. Knucklehead's Knock-Knocks*
(illustrations by Lance Lekander), *Kids' Silliest Knock-Knocks* (illustrations by
Buck Jones), *Ridiculous Knock-Knocks* (illustrations by Mark Zahnd), *Joke &
Riddle Ballyhoo* (illustrations copyright © by Jackie Snider), *Kids' Silliest Jokes*
(illustrations by Buck Jones), *Super Goofy Jokes* (illustrations copyright ©
by Rob Collinet), and *Greatest Goofiest Jokes* (illustrations by Buck Jones).

Sterling ISBN-13: 978-1-4027-4992-6
ISBN-10: 1-4027-4992-9

For information about custom editions, special sales, premium andcorporate
purchases, please contact Sterling Special Sales
Department at 800-805-5489 or specialsales@sterlingpub.com.

contents

1. Starting from Scratch

What does one star say to another star when they meet?

"Glad to meteor."

What did Adam say when Eve fell off the roof?

"Eve's dropping (eavesdropping) again!"

Why did Eve want to move to New York?
She fell for the Big Apple.

What is the moral of the story about Jonah and the whale?
You can't keep a good man down.

Where did money start?
In Noah's ark. The duck had a bill, the lamb had four quarters, the frog had a greenback and the skunk a scent (cent).

9

Who designed Noah's ark?
An ark-itect.

Why was Noah's ark filled with fruit?
Everyone came in pairs (pears).

What did Noah do for people who couldn't get into the ark?

He gave them a rain check.

What did Noah do while spending time on the ark?

He fished, but he didn't catch much. He only had two worms.

What did the musical animals
do on Noah's boat?
They started an arkestra!

Why did Julius Caesar buy
crayons?
He wanted to Mark Antony.

What has ten legs and drools?
Quintuplets.

What do you get between
sunrise and sunset?
Sunburned.

How many days are there in a year?

Seven. Monday, Tuesday, Wednesday, Thursday, Friday, Saturday and Sunday.

What is the best day of the week
to sleep?
Snooze-day.

Where did Columbus land when
he found America?
On the beach!

Who succeeded the first president?
The second one.

What followed the thirteenth president?
His shadow!

Where did Sir Lancelot go to pick up his high school diploma?

Knight school!

When did the dragon finally get full?
Around mid-knight!

What do you call a knight with no home?
A bedless horseman!

Why do dragons sleep all day?
So they can fight knights!

What do you say when you want knights to stop fighting?
"Now, joust a moment!"

What is the most interesting
thing about the word knight?
It has a duel meaning.

What did the suit of armor in the museum miss most?

The knight life!

What did the suit of armor say
after being left out in the rain?
"I think I'll just take a little rust!"

Why do archeologists have so much fun?

Because they really dig their work!

How does the archeologist sing a tune?

"Do Re Mi Fossil-ah Ti Do!"

What do you call it when a pirate digs up a scale?

Buried Measure!

Where is George Washington buried?
Underground!

2. Riddle Me This!

What has four legs but never stands?

A chair!

Here's a riddle as old as the Sphinx! What has four legs, then two, then three?

Man! First he crawls, then he walks, and then he walks with a cane!

Why are Saturday and Sunday stronger than the rest of the week?

The others are all weak days!

What do you call treasure buried under your bed?

Sleeping booty!

What is the fastest growing city in Ireland?

Doublin'!

What shouldn't you ever share with
your friends?
Your cold!

How can you be sure to start a
fire with two sticks?
Make sure one of them is a match.

What starts with e and has only one letter in it?
Envelope!

What makes windows unable to see?
Blinds!

What can one not hold, two pass, and three destroy?
A secret!

Name one thing you can never tell anyone about without making it disappear.

Silence!

Name one thing you can't hold onto for even five minutes?

Your breath!

What has two hands but can't clap?

A watch!

How do you file your taxes?

Under T!

What letter asks too many questions?

y!

Why is it a bad idea to laugh at people when they are down?

They might get up!

Why should you always walk a mile in people's shoes before you criticize them?

Because then you'll be a mile away and you'll have their shoes!

What bow never gets tied?

A rainbow!

What is the least heavy place to live?

In a light house!

Who are the fastest moving people in the world?

The Russians!

Why did the little kid cross the playground?

To get to the other slide!

What gets wet while it dries?

A towel!

Why is Alabama so smart?
Because it has more A's than B's!

What is the worst thing to make
in pottery class?
Mistakes!

What
works best
when it
clenches
its teeth?
A zipper!

What becomes smaller when
you add two letters?
Small!

When is there no room
on the moon?
When it is full!

How does Christmas always end?
With an s!

What bites without using teeth?
Frost!

How do you know cemeteries
will always be popular?
Because people are dying to get in!

Why did the man mail his friend
a clock?
He wanted to see time travel!

3. Sum Tricky Ones!

What did the seven dwarfs bake?
Shortbread!

Twenty sheep, a sheepdog, and a shepherd are in their favorite field. How many feet do they have?
Two! Sheep have hooves and dogs have paws!

What did Mozart become on his thirteenth birthday?
A teenager!

What snake is the best mathematician?
The adder!

Why are math books so hard to get along with?
They have so many problems!

Is it difficult to be impolite?
No, it's rude-a-mentary!

How can you share five apples with seven friends?
Make applesauce!

What did the man who swallowed the dime say to his doctor?
No change yet!

41

You are driving a bus and three children get on at every stop for three stops. At the next two stops, two children get off. At the last stop, three children get on and one gets off. What color are the bus driver's eyes?

Look in the mirror!

What is the best time to go to the dentist?

Around tooth thirty!

Which month has twenty eight days?

They all do!

Why was the boy wearing a jacket and a raincoat to paint the fence?

He was told to put on two coats!

When is it not good to get a hundred on your tests?

When there are two of them!

If you have nine bowling balls in one hand and six in the other, what do you have?

Really big hands!

If there are two umbrellas and five people, how can they avoid getting wet?

By going inside!

What do you get if you divide the number 8 in half?

Two 3s!

If you have two sandwiches and two sodas, what do you have?

Lunch!

What is the difference between India and Africa?

About three thousand miles!

How many seconds are in a year?

Twelve, starting with the second of January!

What kind of plants do math teachers plant?

Ones with square roots!

What has four legs, one trunk, and is gray all over?

A mouse on vacation!

If there are nine flies on a table
and you kill one, how many
are left?

One—the others will fly away!

What do you make bigger by
taking parts away?

A hole in the ground!

What gets bigger the farther away you walk?

Your shadow!

Which is right—six and seven are twelve, or six and seven is twelve?

Neither, six and seven are thirteen!

What table has no legs?
The times table!

A family had three children, all in their teens. The first two were almost 20. How old was the last one?
Third teen!

4. Say What?

Monkey starts with M and finishes with F. How is this possible?

Finishes begins with the letter F!

What antibiotic do you give a sick eraser?

Pencil-in!

What do you get when you cross cola with a bike?

A pop-sicle!

What do you call someone who has been hit by a meteorite?
Starstruck!

Where do you go if you get sick over the rainbow?
To the Oz-pital!

When is it okay to strike a pose?
When it hits you first!

Why should suspenders be wanted by the police?

For holding up your father's pants!

Where do criminal deer end up?
Elk a traz!

What always ends night?
T!

How does morning begin?
With an m!

What landmark has the best view?
The eye-full Tower!

What puzzle is the most dangerous to handle?
The jig saw!

What do computer geeks call a horse's back?
The mane frame!

What's a semaphore?
When you can't afford a whole one!

What room is good for making baby food in?
A mush room!

Can platypuses have babies?
No, they can only have platypuses!

What do you get when you leave tangerines out in the sun?
Orange-u-tans!

How did the seven dwarfs
feel when they got up in
the morning?

*Oh, you know—sleepy, dopey,
grumpy . . .*

Who would have visited the
three bears if she had no hair?

Baldy locks!

Why are Santa's elves always behind in the workshop?

Because they're short-handed!

Why are piñatas never hungry?
Because they're always stuffed!

Why did the glove fall in love?
She met someone hand some!

In the dictionary, what is the shortest month?
It's still February!

Why do pigs have pink skin?
To keep their insides in!

What is the one thing you should take before every meal?
A seat!

5. People Patter

Where do polar bears invest
their money?
In snowbanks.

Who uses voodoo to scare
mosquitoes away?
The itch doctor.

Why did the forest ranger change jobs?

He wanted to turn over a new leaf.

What's a garage mechanic's favorite exercise?
Jumping jacks.

What do you get when you cross a pit bull with a math teacher?

Snappy answers.

MAD ABOUT YOU

Did you hear about the angry
clockmaker?
She was ticked off.

Did you hear about the angry
cloned scientist?
He was beside himself.

Did you hear about the angry
kangaroo?
It was hopping mad.

Did you hear about the angry
bull?
It saw red.

Did you hear about the angry
golfer?
She was teed off.

Why was the king only 12 inches tall?
He was the ruler of his country.

How does a scientist get ready for work?

He puts his genes on.

What's a couch potato's favorite TV show?

M.A.S.H.

What exam must vegetarian lawyers pass before they can practice law?

The salad bar.

What did the lawyer name her daughter?
Sue.

What kind of uniforms do paratroopers wear?
Jump suits.

What did the weatherman say to the grocer?
"I'll take a rain check."

What did the princess say when her photos didn't arrive?
"Someday my prints will come."

Who is the sacred woman
of Tibet?
The Dalai Mama.

What kind of doctor
treats ducks?
A quack.

Why are police officers like
shirtmakers?
They're always making collars.

Why do cats make excellent
maids?
They enjoy a little light mousekeeping.

What's a private detective's favorite vegetable?
A cluecumber.

What does the Lone Ranger use to make up his eyes?
Mask-ara.

Why do undertakers cremate bodies?
To urn their living.

What do garage mechanics wear to ballet class?
Tow shoes.

Where do baby computer programmers like to sit?

On your laptop.

If carpenters measure with yardsticks, what do sailors measure with?

Fishsticks.

Where did Indiana Jones find dinosaur eggs?

On an eggspedition.

What kind of shoes do spies wear?

Sneakers.

What knight never won a battle?
Sir Ender.

What did Silly Billy say to his mean dentist?
"You really hurt my fillings."

Who invented spaghetti?
Someone who used his noodle.

What do lawyers wear to court?

Lawsuits.

What do you get when you cross your right eye with your left eye?

Dizzy.

6. Love's a Funny Thing

What did the frog say to the princess who wouldn't kiss him?

"Warts the matter with you?"

Why are banjos the saddest instrument?

Because people keep picking on them!

Why are violins the happiest instruments?
Because everyone bows before them!

Why are hockey players such good kissers?
They know how to pucker up!

What is the perfect weather for a bride to get married?

Oh, around groom temperature!

What did the duck wear to the wedding?

A duck-seedo!

How did the duck know his wedding was expensive?

He had his bill right in front of him!

Why does everybody love bananas?

Because they're so a-peel-ing!

Where did old soldiers take their wives dancing?

To the Cannon Ball!

What do you call the biggest dance of the winter?
The Snow Ball!

What do you get if you kiss the monkey bars in winter?
Lip stick!

How did the girl know that the letter was from her boyfriend?
It was in the male box!

What flowers have the longest memories?
Forget-me-nots!

"What did you find when you traced your family tree?"
"Termites."

What songs put baby birds
to sleep?
Gull-abies.

Why did the deer's mother wake
her daughter in the morning?
She wanted her doe to rise.

"Where's your brother?"

"Home, playing a duet. I finished first."

85

"Did your baby brother finally stop crying?"

"Yes, my father gave him hush money."

"My father plays the piano by ear. How about yours?"

"Mine fiddles with his moustache."

SNIP

What does a skunk call his
father's brother?
Skunkle.

How did the hot dogs
get married?
For better or wurst.

How did the telephones get married?

In a double ring ceremony.

What government agency finds lost ministers?

The Bureau of Missing Parsons.

What do bullets have when they get married?

Beebies.

How did the pebble's marriage
end up?
On the rocks.

What did one tree say to the
other tree?
"I pine fir yew."

What hog is married to
several wives?
A pig-amist.

7. School Daze

Where do children learn their ABCs?

In LMN-tary school.

What's the difference between school and a mental hospital?

You have to show improvement to get out of the hospital.

What do you call someone who squeals to the teacher?
A school (stool) pigeon.

How did the giraffe do in school?

He got high honors.

What author is known for his very large vocabulary?
Webster.

What school game can you play by yourself?
Hookey.

What is the swine's favorite
subject in school?

Pig-onometry.

What is the moth's favorite
subject in school?

Moth-ematics.

What has a foot on each end and one in the middle?

A yardstick.

What's the difference between one yard and two yards?
A fence.

What contest did the skunk win in school?
The smelling bee.

Did the India Rubber Man pass the test?

Yes, it was a snap.

When will the alphabet have 24 letters?

When U and I are gone.

What country has the largest population of male deer?

Stag-nation.

Why did the college give the baby ghost a scholarship?

It wanted the school to have a little spirit.

How did the thermometer graduate from college?

By degrees.

What did the hen study in college?

Egg-onomics.

What did one cannibal say to the other cannibal at the college reunion?

"How did you like the grads-u-ate?"

What word is always spelled incorrectly?
Incorrectly.

What do you get if you cross a
termite with a book?
An insect that eats its own words.

industrious.
i-n-d-u-s-t...

What is a music teacher noted for?

Sound advice.

When are teachers well liked?
When they have lots of class.

What do students do when they come home from barber school?
Their comb work.

What do dogs do once they're through with Obedience School?
Go for their Masters.

Why did the milk carton sleep in the library?
It wanted to curdle up with a good book.

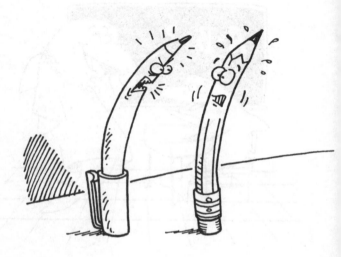

What did the pencil say to the paper?

"I dot my I's on you."

Why should you take a pen to the garden?
So you can weed and write.

What should you do if your baby brother is chewing up your favorite book?
Take the words right out of his mouth.

What did the librarian use for bait?
A bookworm.

Which letters of the alphabet have wings?
Bs and Js.

Why was Silly Billy afraid to go to school?
He had class-trophobia.

What's the only word in the dictionary always pronounced incorrectly?
Incorrectly.

What's a dog called that runs a book company?
A pup-lisher.

Why was the polar bear upset with her test grade?
It was 20 below zero.

What's filled with ink and has no hair?
A bald-point pen.

Where do you go to take a class in making desserts?
Sundae school.

What knight writes at a round table?
King Author.

When does seven come before six?
In the dictionary.

What word has the most letters in it?
Mailbox.

What do you call a teacher who makes numbers disappear?
A mathemagician.

What's a teacher's favorite food?
Graded cheese.

How do wasps communicate on their computers?
By bee-mail.

What did the pen say to the pencil?
"So what's your point?"

Why did the computer squeak?
Someone stepped on its mouse.

What kind of puzzles do toads like?

Crosswarts.

What do plants in your math class grow?

Square roots.

How did the lettuce get an A on the test?

It used its head.

Why does your teacher wear sunglasses?

Because her class is so bright.

What should you do if you get a
B on your math test?
Be careful it doesn't sting you.

8. A Few Odd Jobs...

What did the dentist say to the duck?

"Down in the mouth?"

What did the newspaperman say to defend his strong views?

"Hey, I column as I sees 'em!"

How do you know the seven dwarfs are in debt?

Because they sing, "I owe, I owe, it's off to work I go!"

How do doctors sneak up to check your heartbeat?
With a stealthoscope!

Who do fish doctors pay attention to?
The sturgeon general!

What did the dentist say to the liar who wouldn't show his cavity?
"Tell me the tooth!"

Why did the gardener think he was going nuts?
He heard the beanstalk!

What hero delivers meals to your house?
Supperman!

What is a boxer's favorite beverage?
Punch!

What did the doctor tell the slumping man?

"Watch your stoop!"

Why do performers like to visit prisons?

They love a captive audience!

What is the dentist's favorite animal?

The molar bear!

What does the seventy-five kilo-gram butcher weigh in pounds?

Meat!

What did the plastic surgeon say to the duck?

"I'm going to have to re-bill you!"

Why did the contractor put his size twelve feet in the fresh concrete?

He wanted to make a big impression!

Why do farmers make
great tailors?
**Because they know
how to sow!**

How do you know that the
funeral director has a cold?
You can tell by all the coffin!

What driver goes around in circles?
A screwdriver!

What driver puts screws in a
glass-bottom boat?
A scuba driver!

Why did the zookeeper hate clothes shopping for her animals?

She couldn't get anything to fit over her hippos!

What kind of jewelry do climbers like?

Mountain earring!

How do you unlock the secrets of music?

With piano keys!

If you have a hole in your pocket and you take your pants to the tailor, what do you tell him you need?
Pocket change!

What kind of music do Santa's elves listen to every Christmas Eve?

Wrap!

What do housekeeper rodents do?

Mousework!

What do astronomers sing in the bath?

"When you wash upon a star!"

Who marries every Sunday and still lives alone?

The priest!

127

Where does every locksmith want to live?
The Florida Keys!

What letter is always surprised?
G!

Where do you go when you can't time an egg with your watch?
The second hand shop!

What song do cowboy pilots sing?
"Home, home on the plane!"

Where did the computer stay
when he joined the Army?

At a data base.

What's the difference between a
sailor and a jeweler?

*One watches the sea and the other
sees the watches.*

What did the sailor say
after he became a
computer programmer?

"Don't give up the
chip."

Why did the silly kid buy a
thousand pickles?
He got a good dill.

How did the farmer fix
his jeans?
With a cabbage patch.

What kind of button won't you
find in a tailor shop?
A bellybutton.

What do you call a tailor who
squeals on people?
A spool pigeon.

What is the difference between a
tailor and a salesman?

*A tailor deals in clothes and a
salesman closes deals.*

What's the difference between a man with a cold and a prizefighter?

One blows his nose and the other knows his blows.

What would you get if you crossed a baker with a prizefighter?

A bread box-er.

What did the grouchy baker make?

Crab cakes.

Where do the best bakers live?

On the Yeast Coast.

What does an auto mechanic charge to fix a tire?

A flat rate.

How did the glass worker talk about his work?

He gave a blow-by-blow description.

What is the difference between a submarine and a plumbing supply house?

A submarine sinks ships and a plumbing supply house ships sinks.

How does a plumber feel as he finishes his job?

Flushed.

What happened to the worker at the fence factory?

He got the gate.

How far did the restaurant owner go in his education?
Through deli-mentary school.

What bird never goes to a barber?
A bald eagle.

"Why did you get rid of your watchdog?"
"It couldn't tell time."

Which branch of the military does the most bragging?
The Boast Guard.

Where did the kitten get a job?
On a mews-paper.

If a dog bought a newspaper business, what would he be called?

A pup-lisher.

Why did the duck lose his job?
His company was down-sized.

Why did the trombone player go broke?

He let things slide.

What would you get if you crossed a mathematician with a dentist?

A square root canal.

How do roofers march in a parade?
In shingle file.

What did the janitor do when he became the boss?

He made sweeping changes.

What would you get if you crossed a comedian with a termite?

A joker who brings down the house.

Why did the comedian give up his job?

He was getting jest (chest) pains.

Why does the shoe work seven days a week?

It's the sole support of its family.

How does a leopard examine his bank records?

He does a spot check.

Did you hear about the moon that was broke?

It was down to its last quarter.

What stories do the ship captain's kids like to hear?

Ferry tales.

What's the difference between the captain of a ship and a soft-hearted judge?

One rules the waves and the other waives the rules.

Why was the locksmith so nervous?

He got all keyed up.

9. Take Two Aspirins

Why did the axe go to the doctor?

For a splitting headache.

Why did the horse go to the doctor?

For hay fever.

"How do you know the teacher has a glass eye?"
"It came out in conversation."

What would you get if you crossed an elephant with a skin doctor?

A pachy-dermatologist.

Why did the elephant jump up and down?

He took his medicine and forgot to shake the bottle.

Why did the Chinese cook see his psychiatrist?

He was going off his wok-er.

Why did Chiquita Banana go to see a psychiatrist?

She had a banana split personality.

How did the fish get its nose fixed?

It went to a plastic sturgeon.

What would you get if you crossed a doctor with a hyena?
A physician who laughs all the way to the bank.

What symptoms did the hot charcoal complain about?
Glowing pains.

What's the matter with the blackbird?
It has crowing pains.

What did one ball of twine say to the other ball of twine?
"I'm at the end of my rope."

What disease do witches suffer from?

Broom-atism.

How does the King of the Jungle take his medicine?

Lion (lying) down.

What happened to the man who was sawed in half by the magician?

He hasn't been feeling himself.

Why did the king go to the
dentist?
To get his teeth crowned.

Why did the tree see the dentist?
To get a root canal.

What did the tree say when he saw the tree surgeon?

"Everybody wants to get into the axe (act)."

How come the man died when he was shot in the finger?

He was scratching his head at the time.

Where does a rabbit go to have his eyes examined?

To a hop-tometrist.

What happened when the centipede broke all his feet?

He didn't have a leg to stand on.

What did the tailor take for his sore throat?

Cuff drops.

What does an elephant take for a running nose?

A case of Kleenex.

How do you prevent a summer cold?

Catch it in the winter.

What sickness can you catch from your mattress?

Spring fever.

Why did the fish go to the doctor?
It had a haddock (headache).

What does a snake take for a
headache?
Asp-irin

10. Are We There Yet?

Why do elephants have trunks?
They'd look silly with suitcases on their faces.

What kind of car does a cow drive?
A Cattle-ac.

What kind of bus do fleas take on vacation?
A Greyhound.

PACK YOUR BAGGIES

What does the Sandman pack
his clothes in?
A nap-sack.

What does a reporter pack her
clothes in?
A paper bag.

What do boxers pack their
clothes in?
Sluggage.

What do parachute jumpers
pack their gear in?
Air bags.

How can you tell if a train has just gone by?
You can see its tracks.

Why is a junk car like a baby?
It never goes anywhere without a rattle.

Why did the bus driver go broke?

He drove all his customers away.

Au Revoir

Why did the little Volkswagen cry on the way to the repair shop?
It had to go where it was towed to.

What makes taxi cabs sweet and sticky?
Traffic jam.

What does Tom do when he's driving to the movie studio?
Sets the Cruise control.

How does a duck change a
flat tire?
With a quacker jack.

How do rabbits travel
on vacation?
On TransWorld
Hare-lines.

Where do working bees travel?
On buzzzzzzness trips.

Where do chickens go on
vacation?
Sandy Egg-o.

Where do ducks go on vacation?
Alba-quacky, New Mexico.

Where do termites vacation?
In Holly-wood.

What country makes you shiver?
Chile.

What's purple and 5,000 miles long?
The Grape Wall of China.

What's the weather like in
Mexico City?
Chili today and hot tamale.

What did Silly Sarah think of the Grand Canyon?

That it was just gorges.

Where are the Great Plains?

At the great airports.

What's black and white and lives in Bermuda?

A lost penguin.

What speaks every language?

An echo.

What do you say to a skeleton
going on a cruise?
"Bone Voyage!"

Why can't hobos take
boat trips?
Because beggars can't
be cruisers.

Why can't you play cards on a cruise?

Because the passengers sit on all the decks.

What kind of lettuce do you get on an Alaskan cruise?

Iceberg.

What does a pine tree wear on an Alaskan cruise?

Its fir coat.

Why did the mummy go on a cruise?

It needed a place to unwind.

Where do shellfish sleep on a cruise?

In their crab-ins.

Where does Tiger Woods take a cruise?

In the Golf of Mexico.

Why is the letter "t" like an island?

It's in the middle of water.

What keys won't fit in any door?

The Florida Keys.

Why was there a box of tissue in the hotel elevator?

It was coming down with something.

What happens to a frog's car when the meter expires?

It gets toad away.

What do clowns do when they get into a car?

Chuckle-up.

Why was the auto mechanic fired?

He took too many brakes.

How does a kangaroo start its car if the battery's dead?

With jumper cables.

What did the jack say to the car?

"Need a lift?"

What do you get when it rains on your convertible?

A carpool.

Where do old bicycle tires go?

To the old spokes home.

What happened when dinosaurs started driving?

They had tyrannosaurus wrecks.

Why was the bridesmaid arrested during the wedding?
For holding up a train.

Why did Silly Billy stare at the auto's radio?
He wanted to watch car tunes.

When do frogs take a vacation?
In a leap year.

Where do chickens get off the highway?
At the eggs-it.

Where do lawnmowers fill up?
At the grass station.

11. Long Time, No Sea

What do bumblebees wear on the beach?

Bee-kinis.

What do chickens collect on the beach?

Egg shells.

What happens to a Barbie doll if you leave her out in the sun too long?

She gets Barbie-cued.

What does a shark get when it swallows your computer?

A megabite.

OCEAN SPRAYS

What did the ocean say to the sand?
"How ya dune?"

What did the ocean say to the oyster?
"What time do you open up?"

What did the ocean say to the pier?
"There's something fishy going on here."

Where do goblins
like to cruise?
From ghost to ghost.

What day of the week
do fish hate most?
Fry-day.

Why don't elephants like the
beach?
*They always get sand in their
trunks.*

How does Neptune keep his
underwater castle clean?
He hires mer-maids.

SCUBA-DOO

Why do scuba divers say grace underwater?
Because they're so tank-ful.

When do scuba divers sleep underwater?
When they're wearing their snore-kels.

What should you use if your scuba mask falls apart?
Masking tape.

Why can't whales keep secrets?
They're blubber-mouths.

Why do fish go after worms?
Because they're hooked on them.

What kind of fish growls?
A bear-acuda.

Who should you call if you want to square dance on the beach?
The fiddler crabs.

How did Silly Sarah get rescued from the undertow?
She dialed 911 on her shellular phone.

How do lobsters get to the airport?
By taxi crab.

Why should you build a moat around your sandcastle?

For the moat-er boats.

What do rain clouds wear under their raincoats?

Thunderwear.

What happened after Sammy Seagull broke up with Samantha Seagull?

He found a new gull-friend.

What kind of pictures do sailors paint?

Watercolors.

When are sailors fired?
When the captain wants a crew-cut.

What kind of ship can last forever?
Friend-ship.

What do you get if the Three Blind Mice fall into the Arctic Ocean?
Mice cubes.

What do you call the tiny streams that flow into the Nile?
Juve-niles.

What is the national homeland for fish?

Fin-land.

Which fish is the most dangerous at poker?

The card shark!

Where do down-on-their-luck fishes end up?
Squid Row!

Why are fish so easy to weigh?
They come with their own scales!

What lullaby do you sing to a fish?
"Salmon Chanted Evening!"

Who is always in its house, no matter where it goes?
A turtle!

What do the smartest frogs say?
"Read-it, Read-it!"

What kind of music do funky
fish listen to?
Sole music!

Why did the man say hello to the ocean?

Because it waved at him!

What did the creatures of the sea avoid—two by two?

Noah's shark!

Where do fishes borrow money?
At the river bank!

How did the boat know things weren't going well?
It had that sinking feeling!

Which boat is the smartest?
The scholar ship!

What did the captain say to the tired crew who was heading too far east?
"Why don't you take a little west?"

12. Wild and Woolly

What's the first thing a gorilla learns at school?

His Ape-B-Cs.

What kind of ape lives in a gym?

A gympanzee.

Where do purple monkeys rule the world?

On the Planet of the Grapes.

What kind of monkey can fly?

A hot-air baboon.

What happened to the wild pig
that broke out of the zoo?
They put it in hamcuffs.

Who is a pig's favorite relative?
Its oink-ul.

What lizard wears a hairpiece?
A wiguana.

What kind of bikes do polar bears ride?
Ice-cycles.

What kind of bear loves to play in the rain?

A drizzly bear.

Why do elephants have wrinkled skin?

It's too hard to iron.

Why are lions holy creatures?

They're always preying.

When is it safe to touch a lion?

When it's a dande-lion.

What has a long neck that smells good?
A giraffodil.

Why is it so cheap to feed a giraffe?
A little food goes a long way.

Why can't leopards escape
from the zoo?
*They're always spotted running
away.*

When can a horse leave the
hospital and go home?
When it's in stable condition.

What do you call a chilly donkey?
A brrrr-o.

Who heads the Canine Mafia?
The Dogfather.

Why are camels so hard to see?
They wear camel-flage.

In which month do beavers cut down trees?

Sep-timber.

Why do beavers love sequoia trees?

Because they're totally gnawsome.

What do you get when a hippopotamus plays in your room?

A hippopota-mess.

Why did the ram run off
the cliff?
It missed the ewe turn.

What do you get when you cross
a snake with a kangaroo?
A jump rope.

Why should you rush a frog to
the emergency room?
It could croak at any moment.

Where do sick kangaroos go?
To the hopsital.

What bird is always out of breath?

A puffin.

Which birds help build bridges?

Cranes.

What did the little canary say when her date asked her to go dutch?

"Cheep, cheep."

What bird gulps the loudest?

The swallow!

Why do geese fly south every year?

Because it would take them forever to walk!

What soda do frogs like best?
Cherry croak!

What kind of shoes do frogs
wear on vacation?
Open toad sandals!

Why are owls so much fun?
*Because they're a real hoot to be
around!*

While the mother owl is at work, who takes care of her children?

The hoot-en-nanny, of course!

Of all the big cats, which one can't you ever trust?

The cheetah!

What did the cheetah say when he was accused of telling lies?

"You have to believe me! I'm not lion!"

How do lions do their shopping?
From cat-alogues!

Why are leopards easier to see than jaguars?

Because you can always spot a leopard!

What did the antelope say when he read the paper?

"That's gnus to me!"

What do you call a bear with no shoes?

Bear foot!

What did the mother kangaroo give birth to?

A bouncing baby!

Why do people think skunks are stupid?

Because they never use good scents!

Why are elephants so cheap?
They get paid peanuts!

What feathered creature is the
most sarcastic of all flying
beasts?
The mocking bird!

What is the orangutan's favorite tool?
The monkey wrench!

How do rabbits toast each other?

"Hare's to you!"

What do you call a squirrel who is crazy for chocolate?

Cocoa nut!

What did the man say when he heard the story about the giraffe's hindquarters?

"Now that's a tall tail!"

What did the buffalo say to his child when he went to work in the morning?

"Bison!"

How do you stop a wild boar
from charging?
Take away its credit card!

Who are the smartest insects?
Spelling bees!

Where do insects dance?
At the moth ball!

Whom did the moth take to the ball?
An old flame!

Why was the fly so upset at the newlywed spiders?
He wasn't invited to the webbing!

What was the spider charged with by the bug police?
Assault with a lethal webbin!

What insect has the least courage?
The flee!

What do insects use to hold up
their porches?
Cater pillars!

Who is the clumsiest bee in the hive?
The stumble bee!

What buzz can you barely
understand?
A mumble bee's!

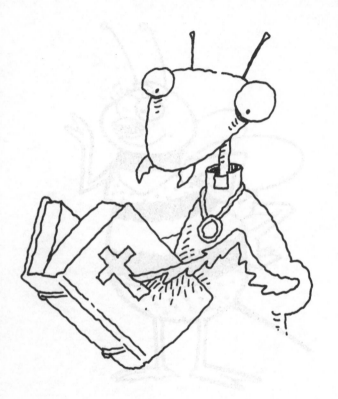

Who never makes the insect football team?
The fumble bee!

What is the bees' favorite musical?
"Stinging in the rain!"

Who is the most religious insect?
The praying mantis!

Where should you look to find out about Lyme disease?
In the tick-tionary!

218

13. Down on the Funny Farm

What animal always has a sore throat?

A horse!

What kind of book is Black Beauty?

A ponytail!

What kind of bad dream did the horse wake up from?

A night mare, of course!

What do you call a legless cow?
Ground beef!

What do you call a sleeping cow
with horns?
A bull dozer!

What do you get from a cow
after an earthquake?
A milkshake!

What do you get from Arctic cows?

Cold cream!

What did the man say to the woman who put her offspring out to pasture?

"Children should be seen, not herd!"

Why did the farmer take his chickens to the vet?

It was time for their rooster shots!

Why did the bubblegum cross the road?

It was stuck on the chicken's foot.

What do you call a chicken that makes funny yolks?

A comedi-hen!

Why did the turkey cross the road?

To prove he wasn't chicken!

How do chickens stay in shape?

With plenty of eggcersize!

Why was the newborn bird so afraid?

He was a little chicken!

Why aren't chickens allowed to speak?
Because they use fowl language!

What did the baby chick say about being born?
"It's not all it's cracked up to be!"

When is the best day to eat eggs?
Fry day!

What part of a vegetable listens best?
An ear of corn!

What loves to bite even though
it only has one row of teeth?
A saw!

Why should you never tell
secrets to pigs?
Because they are bound to squeal!

What do cats like in their drinks on hot days?

Mice cubes!

How do cats stop their favorite videos?

They put them on paws!

What do you feed a cat who yowls all night long?

Tune-a-fish!

What kind of feline can't you ever trust?

A copycat!

227

What kind of dogs always get into fights?
Boxers!

Which dog is the most boring?
The poo-dull!

Where do dogs love to hang out?
In the barking lot!

What animal can always tell you the time?

A watchdog!

What is a dog's favorite vegetable?

Pup-corn!

Where is the one place a dog can't shop?

A flea market!

What is the dog that loves to be washed?

The shampoodle!

Why do cowboys love dachshunds?

They like to get a long, little doggie!

14. Garden Goofies

What vegetable do chickens
grow in their gardens?
Eggplant.

Why should you bury your
money in the garden?
To make the soil rich.

What's a ghost's favorite plant?
Bam-BOO!

What flowers grow
right under your nose?
Tulips.

Why are May flowers so clean?

From all the April showers.

What holiday do cornstalks celebrate every summer?
Happy New Ear.

What fruit is always in a bad mood?
The crab apple.

How do you fix a pumpkin?
With a pumpkin patch.

What vegetable do you get when a dinosaur tromps through your garden?
Squash.

What comes aftercucumbers?
R-cumbers.

What's the most environmentally safe fuel?
Aspara-gas.

What happened when Mama Rabbit was chased out of the farmer's garden?

She didn't carrot all.

Where do vegetables go to get married?

To the Justice of the Peas.

What do vegetables give each other when they get married?
Onion rings.

Why did the grapefruit fall in love with the banana?
The banana had ap-peel.

What do most people think about the centers of cherries?
They're the pits.

What did the snail say when it
hitched a ride on a turtle?
"Wheee!"

What does Santa do
in his garden?
Hoe-hoe-hoe.

Which garden insects are always
polite?
Lady bugs.

Why should lightning bugs
apply to college?
Because they're very bright.

What kind of monkeys are
found in flower gardens?
Chim-pansies.

What kind of bees are found in dead flower gardens?

Zom-bees.

What do mosquitoes learn in art class?

How to draw blood.

What do you call a mosquito riding on your arm?

An itch-hiker.

What do garden snakes do after a fight?

Hiss and make up.

Why are gardeners good quilters?
They like to sow.

How can you recognize a dogwood tree?

By its bark.

How do trees like their ice cream served?

In a pine cone.

What is the best smelling part of a rose?

The scent-er!

What do you call an eager fruit?
Peachy keen!

How do you groom a Christmas tree?

With a pine comb!

15. What's Eating You?

What is a parrot's favorite food?
Macaw-roni.

What kind of food does a race horse eat?
Fast food.

What would you get if you crossed an egg with an ox?

An egg with double yokes (yolks).

What do Eskimos eat for breakfast?

Ice Krispies.

What does a gambler eat for breakfast?

Dice Krispies.

What does a comedian eat for breakfast?

Pun-cakes.

How do you make an artichoke?

Strangle it.

How do you get milk from an elephant?

Open its refrigerator.

What did one refrigerator say to the other refrigerator?

"Have an ice day."

What can you pick in the garden that you can't eat?
A guitar.

What is a caveman's favorite lunch?
A club sandwich.

Where does a snail eat?
In a slow food restaurant.

How does a scuba diver eat?
He sinks (sings) for his supper.

What's the best day to have a
stick of gum?
Chews-day.

What kind of coffee does a cow
drink?
De calf (decaf).

What do policemen eat in Chinese restaurants?
Cop-suey.

How were the hamburgers taken to the police station?
In a patty wagon.

Where does sour cream come from?
Discontented cows.

What are witches' favorite desserts?
Ice cream crones.

How do you make dough rise?
Play the national anthem.

What dessert does the orchestra
eat at Christmas time?
Flute-cake (fruitcake).

What would you get if you crossed a wrestler with a piece of pastry?

Grapple pie.

What did the oyster say as he was eaten by the minister?

"I always wanted to enter the clergy."

Is a clam ever generous?

No, it's always shell-fish.

How did the frog feel after his fifth cup of coffee?
A little jumpy!

What cookie do you eat before lying down in the afternoon?
A nap snack!

Why didn't the moon
eat dessert?
It was full!

What dessert should you always
eat sitting down?
Chair-ee pie!

Where does ketchup stay before it appears in commercials?
In the dressing room, of course!

Why did the man take the job at the bakery?
Because he kneaded the dough!

How did the cup and the saucer feel about the shoddy way they had been washed?

They thought it was dish-picable!

What is the worst tasting drink of the day?

Nas-tea!

What did the potatoes say after the big vote?

"The eyes have it!"

What do you call it when you can't have dessert until after dinner?

Choco-late!

HE HE HE HE HE HE!!!

What would you be if you crossed a fruit with a dog?
Melon-collie!

Where do baby cows go to eat lunch?
The calf-a-teria!

What do you say to a sulky grape?
"Quit your wining!"

What is a tree's
favorite soft drink?
Root beer.

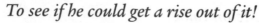

Why did the baker
taunt the bread?
To see if he could get a rise out of it!

How do we know the chef is mean?

We caught him beating the eggs!

How do we know the chef
is nasty?
We saw him whipping the cream!

What is a carpenter's favorite
dessert?
Pound cake!

What kind of picnics do
dentists have?
Toothpick-nics.

What do cats carry to picnics?
Mice chests.

What's the best animal to take along on a picnic?

An anteater.

Why did the truck driver stop on the highway to eat his potato salad?

He saw a fork in the road.

GRILL-A MY DREAMS

What does Dracula grill at a picnic?
Stake.

What does Zorro grill at a picnic?
Sword-fish.

What does an animal keeper grill at a picnic?
Zoo-chini.

What does an angel grill at a picnic?
Wings.

What does a skeleton grill at a picnic?
Ribs.

Why did the jar of mustard burst out crying during the race?

It couldn't ketchup.

Which baseball player is great at pouring lemonade?

The pitcher.

What kind of snack do astronauts take on picnics?

Space-chips.

What do cows put on their hot dogs?
Moo-stard.

Why do dogs like to eat at Italian restaurants?
For the paws-ta.

Where can you leave your dog when you go into a restaurant?
In the barking lot.

What's a rattlesnake's favorite holiday?
Fangs-giving.

What does Jaws order at a restaurant?
Chef Salad.

Why can't you take a turkey out for dinner?
It gobbles its food.

Why did Silly Billy order a large plate of shellfish?
He wanted big mussels.

What snack does the Easter Bunny leave in your navel?
Belly beans.

16. Sports Snorts

What is the insects' favorite sport?
Cricket!

What is harder to catch, the faster you run?
Your breath!

What did the gloomy skier say when he got off the lift?
"It's all downhill from here!"

Why are the players so hot after a basketball game?
All the fans are gone!

What stories are told about basketball stars?
Tall tales!

What is an elephant's favorite sport?
Squash!

Why do bikes need kickstands?
Because they're two tired!

Why did the coach have to go to the bank before the big game?

To get his quarter back!

Where do baseball players always strike out?

The Umpire State Building!

Why are baseball players excellent bakers?

Because they make such good batters!

Why was the baseball player so proud of the cellar of his new house?

It was his first base-ment!

When do hens play hockey?

When they have the chicken pucks.

Why are spiders good baseball players?
They catch lots of flies.

What do you win at the Arctic Olympics?
Cold medals.

How do scientists know cavemen played golf?
They always carried their clubs.

Why don't fortune-tellers go bowling?

Crystal balls don't have finger-holes.

Why do basketball players have to wear bibs?

They dribble all over the court.

Why did the judge become a basketball player?

The court was bigger.

What does a basketball team do for breakfast?

Dunk donuts.

Why can't golfers attend college?

They can only count up to "Fore!"

Where do volleyball players go to dance?
To the beach ball.

Why can't fish play volleyball?
They won't go near the net.

Why didn't Noah do too much fishing on the ark? **He only had two worms.**

Why can't Batman and Robin
go fishing?
Robin eats all the worms.

Why did the football team have
a baby ghost for a mascot?
It needed a little team spirit.

Why did Silly Billy think he'd do
so well on the football team?
Because he had athlete's foot.

Why was the hockey player
successful?
He always aimed for his goals.

WHAT'S THEIR GAME?

What's a baker's favorite game?
Pat-a-cake.

What's a sculptor's favorite game?
Marbles.

What's Mickey Mouse's favorite game?
Hide and Squeak.

What's a weatherman's favorite game?
Twister.

What's a ballet dancer's favorite game?
Tic-tac-toe.

What's a boxer's favorite part of a joke?

The punch line.

Why was the martial arts expert sick?

He had Kung Flu.

What's a runner's favorite subject in school?

Jog-raphy.

Why aren't pigs allowed to play soccer?

They always hog the ball.

Where does a catcher keep his mitt?

In the glove compartment.

Where does the catcher sit at the dinner table?

Behind the plate.

What did the glove say to the baseball?

"Catch you later!"

What is a tennis player's favorite city?
Volley-wood.

What kind of bell never rings?

A barbell.

What position would a ghoul play on a hockey team?

Ghoul keeper.

17. Sym-phony

Why did Silly
Sarah quit
ballet class?
It was tutu hard.

Why are horses
terrible
dancers?
They have two left feet.

How do baby chicks dance?
Cheep-to-cheep.

Where does Tiger Woods go to dance?

The golf ball.

DANCE WITH ME

What kind of dancing do pirates love?
The rum-ba.

What kind of dancing do geometry teachers love?
Square dancing.

What kind of dancing do owls love?
The whoo-la.

Where do rabbits go to hear singing?
The hopera.

Who are the cleanest opera singers?
Soap-ranos.

Why was the opera
singer arrested?
**She was always
breaking into song.**

Who sings slightly lower than
a tenor?
A niner.

Why did the stage manager put
paste on the programs?
*So the audience would be glued to
their seats.*

Why did they let the turkey join the band?
He had the drum-sticks.

Where do hurricanes sit during band practice?
In the wind section.

What instrument do lighthouse keepers play?
Fog horns.

Where do pigs play their violins?
In the pork-estra.

What happens to a harp when its strings break?

It has open-harp surgery.

Why did the shy conductor stand with his back to the orchestra?

He couldn't face the music.

What's an orchestra conductor's favorite dessert?
Cello pudding.

What instrument do dogs love to play?
The trom-bone.

What music do baby bees like?
A Bee CD.

What is a ghost's favorite music?
Spirit-uals.

What is a fashion designer's favorite music?
Rag-time.

What is a termite's favorite instrument?
A wood-wind.

How do musicians march in a parade?
Tuba two.

What instrument can you play even if you can't play music?

You can always blow your own horn.

Why should you study your music lesson before crossing a busy street?

If you don't C-sharp, you will B-flat.

What's a chicken's favorite movie rental store?

Bok-bok-bok-buster.

Why was the movie star ordered off the set?

He was acting up and making a scene.

What did the famous movie star dog do after its performance?

Took a bow-wow.

Why was the actor ordered off the set of Gladiator?

He couldn't remember his lions.

18. It's Fun-damental!

Why did the deer take the elephant to the party?

It was going stag.

Do deer enjoy themselves at parties?

Yes, they have a lot of faun.

Why didn't the hatchet go to the party?
It wasn't axed.

When do people who yell a lot celebrate?

On holler-days (holidays).

What is a soldier's favorite holiday?

Tanks-giving.

What is the best day to ride in a boat?

Cruise-day.

What is the best day to tell jokes?

Pun-day.

What's the favorite day for fathers?
Dad-urday.

What sickness did Santa get going down the chimney?
The flu (flue).

What would you get if you crossed Kris Kringle with a bandage?
Santa Gauze.

What is a gardener's favorite game?
Follow the Weeder.

What is a cannibal's favorite game?
Swallow the Leader.

What is a tree's favorite game?
Follow the Cedar.

What do monsters play at parties?
Hide and freak.

What do snakes play at parties?
Hissing games.

What magazine does a clock read?
Time.

What is a viper's favorite author?
Snake-speare.

What do artists do on their day off?
They take it easel.

What kind of shooting can you do without a camera or a gun?
Para-chuting.

301

What kind of show did the clock have on TV?
A tock (talk) show.

How do hot dog contests come out?

Weiner take all.

How do kittens shop?
From cat-alogues.

How do you honor a chestnut?
Give it a roast.

What is a zombie's favorite day?
Moan-day.

What is a large bird's favorite movie?
"The Wizard of Oz-strich."

19. Crime & Punishment

Why was the weeping willow punished?
For crying out loud.

Why did they arrest the big cheese?
Its alibi was full of holes.

Why did the policeman give the dog a ticket?
For double barking.

Why was the actor arrested?
He stole the show.

Why was the barber arrested?
He had a brush with the law.

How did they catch the gangster who committed the robbery on Mount Everest?

He returned to the scene of the climb.

What kind of birds are most frequently found in captivity?
Jailbirds.

Why did the pencil end up in jail?

It was lead (led) astray?

Why didn't the crooked tailor go to jail?
He mended his ways.

What would you get if you crossed a homing pigeon with a serial killer?

A bird that keeps coming back to the scene of the crime.

What would you get if you crossed a serial killer and a waiter's best customer?

Jack the Tipper.

20. A Monstrosity of Mirth

Why do ghosts go to the opera?
To boo the singers!

Why are ghosts so popular
in class?
They have such good school spirit!

How do ghosts learn to fight?
By shadow boxing!

What do you call a shy vampire?
Bats-ful!

What do trolls call their after-school assignments?

Gnome work!

What did the sign say above the hobbit's hole?

Gnome sweet Gnome!

What do they call the weird sisters at the beach?

Sand-witches!

How did the weird sisters get home after their brooms broke down?

They witchhiked!

What do witches' cats like for breakfast?

Sorcerers of milk!

What do witches like in their coffee?

Scream and sugar!

How did the broom meet his wife?

He swept her off her feet!

What do you call a phony wizard?

Hocus Bogus!

What is the vampires' least favorite food?

Garlic Stake!

What do waiters say when they see a ghost?

"Good evening, sir, how do you boo?"

What do you say to a self-centered giant?

"Oh, get ogre yourself!"

What did the leprechaun find after searching for the end of the rainbow at the North Pole?

A lucky pot of cold!

What kind of vegetable does Big Foot put in his garden?

Sas-squash!

Why didn't the skeleton cross the road?

He was gutless!

21. Totally Nuts

Why doesn't your parrot say what you tell him to?

He believes in freedom of screech.

What animals are the most reckless gamblers?
Cows. They play for big steaks (stakes).

What do you call a story about a cow that has a fairy godmother?
A dairy tale.

On what side of the bed does a cow sleep?
The udder side.

How do you warm up a room after it's been painted?

Give it a second coat.

What did one watch say to the other watch?

"Got a minute?"

Why did the elephant go to the locksmith?
To have his trunk opened.

Is the skunk very talkative?
No, he's a creature of pew (few) words.

How do bees travel?
By buzz (bus).

What people would never join a nudist camp?

Pickpockets.

What side of a house gets the
most rain?
The outside.

What did one ball of twine say
to the other ball of twine?
"Stop stringing me along!"

How does the Abominable Snowman pay its bills?
With cold cash.

Why is the zombie always broke?
Because a ghoul (fool) and its money are soon parted.

324

What did one shoelace say to
the other shoelace?

"This is knot (not) my day."

What did one blackbird say to
the other blackbird?

"Crow up!"

How did the crow
cross the river?

In a crow boat.

How did the gnu cross the river?

In a ca-gnu.

How do you make a weather vane?

Keep giving it compliments.

Why was the broom late?

It overswept.

Why did the elephant grow a beard?

He got tired of cutting himself shaving.

How does a European mountain call for assistance?

"Alp, alp!"

What do you call a talkative monkey?

A blaboon.

What do you call a fussy cat?

Purr-ticular.

What did one lamb say to the other lamb?

"Talk is sheep."

How do dinosaurs apologize?

They say, "I'm dino-saury."

What do you call a person whose car has been repossessed?
A pedestrian.

What exam does an exterminator have to take?
A pest test.

How does a street organist like his job?
It's a grind.

industrious.
i-n-d-u-s-t...

How do acrobats fall in love?
Head over heels.

What kind of hair do oceans have?

Wavy.

What runs but never walks?
Water.

What would you get if you
crossed a weeping willow with
a nun?
A sob sister.

What would you get if you crossed a weeping willow with a UFO?

A crying saucer.

What did the skunk say when he went broke?

"I'm down to my last scent (cent)."

Why is a forest always congested?

Because trees a crowd.

What did one parallel line say to the other parallel line?

"What a shame we'll never meet."

Why did the leopard go to the cleaners?

To have some spots removed.

How do you make a milk shake?
Give it a good scare.

What is a reptile's favorite movie?
"The Lizard of Oz."

What would you get if you crossed a kookaburra with a comedian?

A bird that laughs at its own jokes.

What would you get if you crossed an elephant with a chicken?

The biggest coward in town.

What do bad little wolves become?

Big bad wolves.

What do you call an insect that talks a lot and then turns into a moth?

A chatter-pillar.

Why did the elephant wear pink
suspenders?
It's color blind.

Why did the monster
go to Iceland?
To ghoul (cool) down.

Where do pigs live?
In a high grime area.

How does a mixed-up cat feel?
Purr-plexed.

How does the goat keep his hands warm?
He has kid gloves.

What's the best way to tell people they have bad breath?
By telephone.

What's faster—heat or cold?
Heat—you can always catch a cold.

How do you make a sidewalk?
Take away its car.

What do you say to someone who's sorry the book is over?

Don't worry, you're not riddle me yet!

Index